kid STARS!

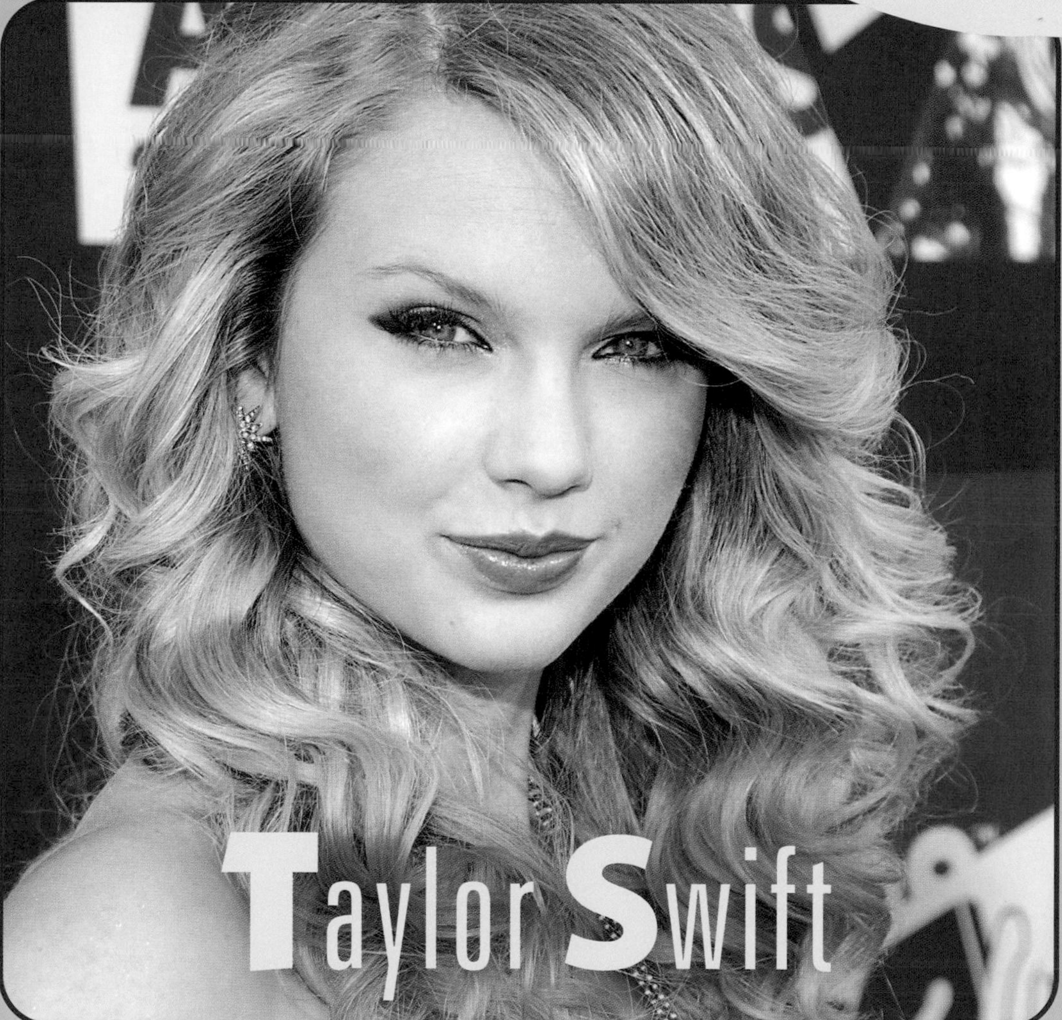

Taylor Swift

Katherine Rawson

PowerKiDS press

New York

jE/B / SWIFT / [Taylor] / Rawson

Published in 2010 by The Rosen Publishing Group, Inc.
29 East 21st Street, New York, NY 10010

First Edition

Editor: Nicole Pristash
Book Design: Kate Laczynski
Book Layout: Julio Gil
Photo Researcher: Jessica Gerweck

Photo Credits: Cover Kevin Mazur/WireImage/Getty Images; p. 4 Sean Gallup/Getty Images; pp. 7, 16, 20 Rick Diamond/WireImage/Getty Images; p. 8 Al Messerschmidt/Getty Images; p. 11 Rusty Russell/Getty Images; p. 12 Kevin Winter/ACMA/Getty Images for ACMA; p. 15 Vince Bucci/Getty Images for AMA; p. 19 Scott Gries/Getty Images.

Library of Congress Cataloging-in-Publication Data

Rawson, Katherine.
  Taylor Swift / Katherine Rawson. — 1st ed.
      p. cm. — (Kid stars!)
  Includes index.
  ISBN 978-1-4042-8138-7 (library binding) — ISBN 978-1-4358-3410-1 (pbk.) — ISBN 978-1-4358-3411-8 (6-pack)
  1. Swift, Taylor, 1989– —Juvenile literature. 2. Women country musicians—United States—Biography—Juvenile literature. I. Title.
  ML3930.S989R39 2010
  782.421642092—dc22
  [B]

                                    2009010464

Manufactured in the United States of America

CPSIA Compliance Information: Batch #WR904211PK: For Further Information contact Rosen Publishing, New York, New York at 1-800-237-9932

Contents

Meet Taylor Swift..5
Country Girl 6
Getting Her Voice Heard 9
Taylor's Big Break 10
Top of the Charts 13
Big Winner..14
Songs About Life 17
Fearless 18
Living Her Dream 21
Fun Facts 22
Glossary..23
Index 24
Web Sites 24

Taylor is a big star in the music business. *Rolling Stone* named her one of the one hundred people who are changing America.

Meet Taylor Swift

Taylor Swift is one of the biggest country-music stars around. She is also one of the youngest. Taylor was only 16 years old when she recorded her first album. It became a big hit, and now she has **millions** of fans around the world.

Taylor has wanted to be a singer since she was young. She has worked hard for her success. Taylor learned how to sing and play the guitar, and she writes her own songs. She is one of the most talented stars in country music today. Here's a look at the life and work of this **popular** young singer!

Country Girl

Taylor Alison Swift was born on December 13, 1989. She grew up in Wyomissing, Pennsylvania. Her mother and father are Andrea and Scott Swift. She has a younger brother named Austin. Taylor comes from a **musical** family. Her grandmother was an **opera** singer.

Taylor started singing at a young age. When she was eight years old, she got a part in the musical *Grease*. In the musical, Taylor sang her songs in a country-music **style**. Singing that way was natural for her. From that point on, Taylor knew that country music was the style of music that she liked best.

Taylor (right) is very close to her mother, Andrea (left). Taylor says that her mom is always there for her.

Taylor has sung "The Star-Spangled Banner" at several sports games. Here she is shown singing it at a Detroit Lions football game in 2006.

Getting Her Voice Heard

Taylor knew that she wanted to be a singer. She entered singing **contests**, and she sang every place she could. Taylor was asked to sing "The Star-Spangled Banner" at a basketball game when she was just 11 years old!

Taylor wanted to make an album. She recorded a tape of herself singing some songs, and she took it to Nashville. Nashville is a city in Tennessee where many country-music singers get their start, and it is an important place in the country-music business. Taylor gave her tape to record companies, and she hoped that the people there would like her voice.

Taylor's Big Break

Taylor soon got her first guitar. She learned to play it, and she started writing her own songs. Taylor often played until her fingers bled! Taylor also made more visits to Nashville, and she met other singers and songwriters there. Finally, her family decided to move to Hendersonville, Tennessee, near Nashville. That made it easier for Taylor to work on her music.

One day, a man named Scott Borchetta saw Taylor sing at the Bluebird Cafe, a famous place for singers in Nashville. Scott had a recording company. He liked Taylor's music, and he asked her to make an album with his company.

Someone once told Taylor that her fingers were too small to play the guitar. Taylor has said, "Anytime someone tells me that I cannot do something, I want to do it more."

Taylor (middle) was very excited to tour with
Faith Hill (left) and Tim McGraw (right). She said working
with them was amazing.

Top of the Charts

In October 2006, Taylor **released** her first album, *Taylor Swift*. One of the songs on the album is called "Tim McGraw." The song became a big hit. Another song from the album, "Teardrops on My Guitar," reached number two on the Billboard Hot Country Songs chart. Then, Taylor's song "Our Song" reached number one!

In the summer of 2007, when she was 17, Taylor went on **tour** with Tim McGraw and Faith Hill, two country singers, on their Soul 2 Soul II tour. They played **concerts** around the country, and Taylor shared her music with many people. Taylor was now becoming famous across America!

 Big Winner

Taylor's first album was very popular. It went triple platinum. This means that more than three million **copies** of the album have been sold! Then, in 2008, Taylor won several music **awards**. Two of those awards were the American Music Award for **Favorite** Female Country Artist and the Teen Choice Award for Breakout Artist.

Taylor had become a big star very quickly. Her music was being played on the radio every day. Taylor was getting new fans, too. Many young people like to listen to her songs because she sings about things that can happen in the lives of people Taylor's age.

Here Taylor is shown getting the American Music Award for Favorite Female Country Artist. The award show took place on November 23, 2008, in Los Angeles.

Taylor's fans connect with her music because Taylor lives a normal life, despite being a star. Taylor often takes time to be with her friends, such as singer Miley Cyrus (right).

Songs About Life

Taylor writes most of her songs by herself. Sometimes, though, she writes with other songwriters. Taylor gets the ideas for her songs from her own life.

Taylor's music is about people she knows and about things that have happened to her. Her song "Tim McGraw" is about an old boyfriend of hers. Taylor has also written a song about her mother and a song about her best friend. She writes about love, boys, and things that happen at school. Young people enjoy Taylor's music because she sings about things that also happen to them. It is easy for Taylor's fans to connect with her songs.

Fearless

Taylor released her second album in November 2008. It is called *Fearless*. A fearless person is not afraid. This is a good name for Taylor's album because she has never been afraid to follow her dream of becoming a singer.

Taylor worked hard to sell *Fearless*. She played concerts and appeared on TV shows to talk about her album.

Fearless was a popular album from the beginning. During the first week of sales, more than 500,000 copies were sold. Taylor was very **excited** when she heard about that. "I never expected this!" she said.

In November 2008, Taylor sang the song "Love Story" from her album *Fearless* at the Country Music Awards, in Nashville.

Taylor has said that she loves when fans want to meet her because she wants to meet them, too! Here she is seen with some of her fans in Nashville.

Living Her Dream

Besides making music, Taylor has been busy doing other things. She has helped create a line of clothes with L.e.i., a clothing brand, to be sold only at Wal-Mart department stores. Music, though, is her number-one love. Taylor wants to continue getting her music to her fans. "Fans are my favorite thing in the world," she has said.

Taylor Swift is living her dream. She wanted to be a singer and a songwriter, and now she is doing those things. Taylor has been a huge success. She hopes to keep on singing and writing songs for many years to come.

TAYLOR SWIFT

 Taylor grew up on a Christmas tree farm in Wyomissing.

 She has two Dobermans and a cat named Indi.

 In her free time, Taylor enjoys baking. Her favorite food is cheesecake.

 Taylor's favorite color is white, and her favorite outfit is a sundress and cowboy boots.

 She loves black-and-white pictures.

 Taylor was homeschooled, and she finished in 2008.

 She has written more than 200 songs. Her favorite thing to write about is love.

 She is friends with country singers Kellie Pickler and Carrie Underwood.

 Taylor has said that she is not good at sports.

 Love Actually is Taylor's favorite movie.

Glossary

awards (uh-WAWRDZ) Special honors given to someone.

concerts (KONT-serts) Musical performances.

contests (KON-tests) Games in which two or more people try to win.

copies (KO-peez) Things that are made to look and sound exactly the same as something else.

excited (ik-SYT-ed) Happy or very interested.

favorite (FAY-vuh-rut) Most liked.

millions (MIL-yunz) Very large numbers.

musical (MYOO-zih-kul) Of or having to do with music.

opera (AH-pruh) A play that is sung to music.

popular (PAH-pyuh-lur) Liked by lots of people.

released (ree-LEESD) Put out for sale.

style (STYL) The way in which something is done.

tour (TUR) When a band or singer travels to different places to play music or sing.

23

Index

A
album, 5, 9–10,
    13–14, 18
awards, 14

C
concerts, 13, 18
country music, 5–6

F
family, 6, 10

fans, 5, 14, 17, 21

G
grandmother, 6
guitar, 5, 10, 13

L
life, 5, 14, 17

S
style, 6

success, 5, 21

T
tour, 13

W
work, 5
world, 5, 21
Wyomissing,
    Pennsylvania,
    6, 22

Web Sites

Due to the changing nature of Internet links, PowerKids Press has developed an online list of Web sites related to the subject of this book. This site is updated regularly. Please use this link to access the list:
www.powerkidslinks.com/kids/swift/